Love, Conflict And Marriage

Guidelines For An Exciting Family Life

Paul H. Eichar

Fairway Press
Lima, Ohio

LOVE, CONFLICT AND MARRIAGE

FIRST EDITION
Copyright © 1993 by
Paul H. Eichar

All rights reserved. No portion of this book may be reproduced or utilized in any form or by any means, electronic or mechanical including photocopying, without permission in writing from the publisher. Inquiries should be addressed to: Fairway Press, 628 South Main Street, Lima, Ohio 45804.

7988 / ISBN 1-55673-589-8   PRINTED IN U.S.A.

My deepest thanks and appreciation to everyone who has contributed to making this booklet a reality. You are known to God and you are known to me. Without your assistance it would not have been possible.

My wife, Joyce, and I, would like to dedicate this booklet to our children and families. We pray they will always have this kind of love for each other that will hold them together and cause peace and joy within their homes.

Miriam is married to Henry Flores, with two step-children, Ray and Ashley.

Elizabeth (Betty) is married to James Zeigler with three children, Jessica, James and John.

Catherine Denise is married to Harold Patterson with two children, Kelly and Daniel.

Jonathan is married to Rosemarie Flores with two children, Joshua and Jordan.

TABLE OF CONTENTS

Introduction	7
Love	11
Eros Love	13
Philio Love	17
Agape Love	19
Partnership	21
Marriage And Family Life	23
The Straight-Line Marriage	24
Raging-Triangle Marriage	24
A Lopsided-Triangle Marriage	25
A Disastrous-Triangle Marriage	26
The Ideal-Triangle Marriage	28
The Ideal-Diamond Marriage	30
A Lopsided-Diamond Marriage	32
The Wedge	33
Wedding Plans	39
Serious Things To Consider Before Divorce	47

INTRODUCTION

Weddings are dramatized and commercialized in such a way one almost feels that peaceful environment surrounding the WEDDING CEREMONY should last forever. The soft melodious music, words spoken filled with love and peace, and so much joy and excitement fill the atmosphere. Many brides and bridegrooms want this kind of MARRIAGE RELATIONSHIP. They want and expect their homes and lives to be filled with this LOVE, JOY, PEACE, AND HARMONY they experienced on their wedding day.

What happens? What in the world goes wrong with marriages? Why are ONE-HALF of the marriages ending in DIVORCE? Why do so many couples discover staying married and maintaining this spirit of LOVE, JOY, PEACE, AND HARMONY SO DIFFICULT TO ACCOMPLISH IN MARRIED LIFE?

I use the word COUPLES because marriages being strained and broken involve not only the young married. People married 10, 20, 30, 40, yes even 50 years are filing for divorce today. That LOVE, JOY, PEACE, AND PERFECT HARMONY that brought couples together are no longer there! I have heard many professional people say, "YOU CAN FALL IN LOVE; YOU CAN FALL OUT OF LOVE!"

We can scream, "NO! NO!" Marriages are for a lifetime! Reality and the increased rate of SEPARATION and

DIVORCE prove to us otherwise. All we need to do is listen to the news, pick up a newspaper, listen to some gossip, and we will soon realize many marriages planned for a lifetime are in serious trouble. A sad commentary also reveals to us that many marriages are nothing more than LITTLE HELLS HERE ON EARTH! For the most part, these are self-made HELLS. Such marriages are filled with fighting, swearing, picking, nagging, tensions and cutting remarks. Sometimes some of these people feel as if they are living in a deep freeze. There is no real communication, just a coldness and a feeling of bitterness.

Somehow husbands and wives have lost that spark which brought them together. They exist as man and wife without any real feelings for each other. The great tragedy about a couple like this is they can put on such a show when they are in public no one would ever expect any internal problems at home.

I was taught in seminary GOOD MARRIAGES DON'T HAPPEN BY CIRCUMSTANCE — YOU MUST WORK AT THEM! This means a couple struggles together, plays together, works together, suffers together, as well as loves and has sex together. Floyd and Harriet Thatcher say it quite well in their book, *Long Term Marriages*, "Marriage is a constant movement; we never arrive, but we are always in the process of becoming." In my 35 plus years in the ministry, I have performed over 500 weddings. What disturbs me greatly is after I have counseled and married a couple, I read or hear they are DIVORCED. Many of them have never come for help or assistance and have not practiced what was shared with them in pre-marital counseling. The symbols on the cover and in this booklet have come out of experience in working with couples going through divorce or being married a second time. They teach us valuable lessons!

I am not saying SEPARATION and DIVORCE are right or wrong, good or bad. What I have learned and know as a fact is that in such a situation there is usually a feeling of bitterness, anger, tears and a tearing of the heart. Yet I agree with many professionals who declare it is common knowledge that, after all other avenues have been explored, SEPARATION OR DIVORCE may be the only way WHOLENESS AND HEALTH CAN RETURN TO A COUPLE! I say this is only when there is NO CHANCE OF RECONCILIATION. Dr. Samuel Johnson years ago observed, "A second marriage represents the triumph of hope over experience." It is common knowledge some professionals feel a second or third marriage has better chances of success.

I do not propose to be the final authority on MARRIAGE AND MARRIAGE PROBLEMS. Neither will you find all of the answers in any one book. It is my purpose to share with you some of the good and bad I have experienced working with people. My prayer would be that you might AVOID SOME OF THE PITFALLS OF MARRIAGE AND THAT YOUR MARRIAGE WILL BE A LONG TERM MARRIAGE FILLED WITH LOVE, JOY, PEACE AND HARMONY.

How can this be done? These following chapters are written to be a help in making your marriage a successful one!

I have been encouraged by so many people preparing for marriage to remind everyone getting married that all third-party people — grandparents, parents, friends — are the ones who cause the lopsided family to develop. This spells disaster in a marriage. This topic is discussed fully in the chapter titled Marriage And Family Life.

LOVE

In today's world LOVE can mean a multitude of things. To a child LOVE could mean an ice cream cone, a puppy dog, a toy, visiting grandparents, going fishing, and so on. Who has not heard a child say, "I love ice cream, I love my puppy, I love my new toy, I love going to grandma's or I love going fishing!"? To a grandparent love could mean grandchildren or security or good health. Have we not heard grandparents say, "I love my grandchildren; I love my property in Florida. I love good health. I love security." I remember being called to the hospital in the middle of the night. On my return home at a city intersection I noticed two young men in their car talking to two young women across the street from them. When I rolled down my window, I heard them talking about the kind of love that was altogether different than we have thus far discussed. It was purely sexual.

A BRIDE AND BRIDEGROOM STAND BEFORE LOVED ONES, FRIENDS, THE CLERGY AND GOD AND TELL THE WHOLE WORLD THEY LOVE EACH OTHER. What in the world are they talking about? Allow me to share with you the MEANING OF LOVE I discovered long ago while I was in seminary. The English language does a horrible job putting a handle on LOVE. It means too many things to too many people. Allow me to share with you THREE GREEK WORDS MEANING LOVE. I am convinced that if these THREE GREEK WORDS could take hold of married couples there would be fewer separations and divorces and families would have homes filled with a lot more LOVE, JOY, PEACE AND HARMONY! Let's look at these three kinds of LOVE.

EROS LOVE

THE GREEK MEANING OF EROS LOVE IS PHYSICAL LOVE AND SEXUAL LOVE! This is the type of love that brings people together. You like the way someone looks! You like to be close to someone, you like to hold hands, you like someone's makeup, his/her perfume, or cologne. EROS LOVE has only to do with the physical side of love. Your looks, holding hands, giving hugs, the way you dress to the sex act itself is all EROS LOVE. This type of LOVE is needed to make any marriage successful.

The astonishing thing about EROS LOVE is this is the only kind of love too many people know or care anything about. As paradoxical as it may sound, this is the first kind of love that will cause DEEP AND COMPLEX PROBLEMS WITHIN YOUR MARRIAGE! Allow me to explain.

A husband does something that irritates his wife. It could be anything from spending money foolishly to looking at another woman. His wife can yell at him and he will laugh at her; she can curse him and he will laugh; she can take her fists and pound him and he will laugh; BUT WHEN THIS WIFE TELLS HIM, "DON'T TOUCH ME!" he suddenly learns EROS LOVE that sounded so good and looked so great and wonderful has suddenly been turned into a WEAPON TO BE USED AGAINST HIM. He is not allowed to touch, hug, hold hands and have sex. That for the moment is completely out of the question. There are a variety of ways a woman can use EROS as a weapon to punish her husband. She can come right out and say, "Not tonight!" She may tell him she is not feeling well. She may not want her hair messed up or it's too late or she's too tired. I'm sure you can add a few to this list if you'd seriously think about it.

The husband does the very same thing to his wife when she does something that irritates him. A husband is a little more sneaky. He stays up and watches the late news or gets involved in a movie or falls asleep on the couch. He makes sure not to go to bed until his wife is asleep. He may tell his wife he has work to do on this or that, but what is he really saying? He is really saying, "DON'T TOUCH ME TONIGHT, SWEETHEART!" See what you have done to EROS LOVE? EROS LOVE has gone out the window. There is no doubt that Eros Love is out of a marriage when one member needlessly sleeps on the couch.

When a husband and wife become irritable or angry with each other the most common way (some women declare, it's the only way they can get their attention) they handle the situation is to TAKE EROS LOVE AWAY. Eros love brings two people together, and if it is mishandled in the marriage, it could well be the instrument used that leads to the end of the marriage!

IT IS A TRAGEDY WHEN SO MANY PEOPLE ENTER INTO A MARRIAGE RELATIONSHIP THINKING ONLY OF LOVE IN TERMS OF EROS! What kind of love is left when Eros Love is removed for an hour or a day or longer?

A.

I want to share a couple of illustrations that will help explain what I am talking about.

A husband and wife, married seven years, walked into a counselor's office. Two chairs were placed side by side for the husband and wife to be seated. When they entered the room, the husband took one chair and moved it to extreme right. His wife took the other chair and moved it to her extreme left.

```
    O  O CHAIRS              O ◄ CHAIRS ►  O
    | DESK |                    | DESK |
```

    The counselor asked what seemed to be their problem? They both agreed there was a problem but had no idea what the problem was. The counselor asked the husband, "Does it have anything to do with SEX?" (EROS LOVE). The husband responded, "WHAT'S THAT?" Immediately the wife came to her own defense. "Well, how am I supposed to feel when my husband stops at the bar on pay day and drinks and gambles most of his check away. We don't have money to buy groceries, and the kids can't have the clothes they need, and we can't pay our bills!" Needless to say they did have problems. What I want you to see is, yes, the husband did a dumb and foolish thing, and, yes, the wife is using the EROS LOVE THAT BROUGHT THESE TWO PEOPLE TOGETHER SEVEN YEARS EARLIER AS A MEANS TO PUNISH HER HUSBAND. SHE FELT JUSTIFIED IN TAKING EROS LOVE AWAY FROM HER HUSBAND.

B.

    The counselor sat in his office on a summer afternoon enjoying the fresh summer breeze from the wide-open windows. He heard a car horn honk next to his office and heard the voices of people, a door slam, and a couple shouts. A few minutes later his neighbor, a young married man, walked into his office and said, "You got to go over and talk to my wife, she locked me out of the house and told me to get lost." (That's the mild way of putting it.) The counselor asked, "What happened?" The young husband told him that he and his wife had been looking for a new car since he had a good job. They had been looking for months. That particular day this young husband and his dad went to town and picked out the car for this young husband and his young wife. The noise and voices the counselor had heard through his windows was when the young husband drove the car into his driveway and honked the horn. When his wife came out, he had said, "LOOK WHAT DAD AND I PICKED OUT FOR US!" THAT IS WHEN SHE SLAMMED THE DOOR, LOCKED IT FROM THE INSIDE, AND TOLD HIM TO GET LOST. The counselor told him he had only made one mistake. He forgot he didn't SLEEP WITH HIS DAD. The counselor discovered the wife wanted to help choose the color, style and make of the car they were going to purchase. EROS LOVE COULD NOT BE FOUND IN THAT HOME FOR A FEW DAYS. DON'T TOUCH ME! SLEEP ON THE SOFA WAS THE ULTIMATUM SHE GAVE HER HUSBAND. ALMOST EVERY HUSBAND AND WIFE CAN THINK OF TIMES WHEN WE HAVE USED EROS LOVE TO SAY "DON'T TOUCH ME!"

PHILIO LOVE

There are two other kinds of LOVE every marriage should possess. The second GREEK WORD meaning LOVE is PHILIO. PHILIO LOVE has a deeper meaning and level of LOVE. Philio love means you care and are concerned. Philio love causes a wife to know her husband cares for her by the way he treats her. She knows he is concerned about her. A husband knows his wife cares about him and is concerned about him by the way she talks and listens and by the very way she treats him. This is what we mean in our marriage vows when we say CHERISH.

The tragedy about this kind of love is that it is not found in all marriages. In many marriages based solely on EROS LOVE, this is MISSING! You don't have to care or be concerned to carry on an EROS LOVE AFFAIR. Prostitution and the flings some people are engaged in are strictly for the physical and sexual pleasure they can get out of it. Many hearts have been broken because one party discovered too late their LOVER only wanted them for SEXUAL REASONS. EROS LOVE ALONE is very close to an animal type LOVE.

Philio Love In Action

A husband and wife have made plans. She was to be home

at 4 p.m. A little after 4 p.m. she called her husband because something unexpected happened and she cared about her husband. She informed him she would not be home until 5:30 p.m. The husband had tickets for a 7 p.m. ball game, 25 miles away. The wife knew all of this. What is this husband going to say to his wife when she gets home? This is what he did. First, he straightened up the house; second, he went out and picked up a snack to eat and fixed it in the oven; third, at 5:25 p.m. he ran the bath water for his wife; fourth, he greeted her at the door, expressed concern about her having such a difficult day and told her the bath water was ready and there was a snack in the oven.

WHY, WOULD ANY MAN DO THIS FOR HIS WIFE? Because he loved her with a PHILIO LOVE. He cared about her. He was concerned about her. She knew he cared and was concerned about her by the way he treated her. They walked hand in hand out the door at 6:10 p.m. and snuggled in their car all the way to the ball game. They snuggled in their seats at the ball game and EROS LOVE WAS IN THEIR BEDROOM WHEN THEY ARRIVED HOME!

LEARN IT NOW! THE MORE PHILIO LOVE A MATE SEES IN YOU AND RECEIVES FROM YOU, THE MORE EROS LOVE YOUR MATE IS GOING TO GIVE YOU. THE LESS PHILIO LOVE A MATE SEES IN YOU THE LESS EROS LOVE YOUR MATE IS GOING TO GIVE YOU.

Remember PHILIO LOVE is a greeting, HI, HELLO, A SMILE, A LISTENING EAR. In fact, it is anything that would tell your mate you care and are concerned about him/her. If all marriages would possess this PHILIO LOVE OR CARING AND BEING CONCERNED FOR ONE ANOTHER, fewer and fewer marriages would end up in the DIVORCE COURTS.

Nothing means more to a wife or a husband than knowing that his/her mate cares and is concerned about them. Demonstrate this kind of love always in your marriage.

AGAIN THE MORE PHILIO LOVE YOU GIVE YOUR MATE, THE MORE EROS LOVE YOU WILL RECEIVE.

AGAPE LOVE

THE THIRD LEVEL OF LOVE IN THE GREEK LANGUAGE IS AGAPE LOVE. This kind of love goes even deeper than PHILIO LOVE. It means you are willing to be UNDERSTANDING AND EVEN MAKE SACRIFICES FOR ONE ANOTHER. The greatest example of AGAPE LOVE is the Christian belief that Jesus Christ, not because he had to, but understanding God's Will, sacrificed himself on the cross for the sin of the world. Not very many of us are going to have to die for one another. There is no reason for it. There is a reason, however, to include AGAPE LOVE in every marriage. Every marriage has times when understanding and making sacrifices for one another must take place. This kind of love must exist when children are born to the union created by marriage.

A wife could become sick suddenly. Her husband would willingly cancel a bowling night, or a fishing trip, or make some other personal sacrifice because he possessed AGAPE LOVE for his wife that included being understanding and making sacrifices for the one he loves.

A wife may want a new wardrobe or a house redecorated or 1,000 other things, and because the bank account can't really handle it, she is willing to be understanding and make some sacrifices too.

THIS IS AGAPE LOVE AND THE MORE AGAPE LOVE IN A MARRIAGE THE MORE EROS LOVE IS GOING TO BE SHARED BY EACH OTHER!

A young couple had come to a counselor to discuss their wedding plans. The counselor discussed with them the three levels of love every marriage should possess. EROS love was discussed, PHILIO love was discussed, and AGAPE love was discussed. The next morning the BRIDE came back to the counselor's office with tears running down her cheeks. She told the counselor she had canceled her wedding. Her BRIDEGROOM told her if she ever expected him to be concerned or make any sacrifices for her because of sickness, pregnancies, or any reason at all, she was sadly mistaken. She could call her mother in times like these! She was to be his SEX MACHINE! That's all he wanted her for! She never dreamed that was the only way he loved her and knew it was better to end the engagement and cancel the wedding than be married to him, have a child, and wind up with a divorce later on down the road.

Agape love is filled with understanding and sacrifices by both parties in a marriage. It needs to be practiced by both husband and wife.

Learn it now and learn it well! The more Agape and Philio love your mate sees in you, the more Eros love your mate is going to share with you. The less Agape love and Philio love your mate sees in you, the less and less Eros love your mate is going to give you.

What I am trying to say is simply this: you need all three kinds of LOVE in your marriage to have a loving, happy, joyful, and long lasting marriage.

EROS LOVE ALONE IS DOOMED TO FAIL. It is used to punish and hurt as well as to love.

YOU NEED PHILIO LOVE IN YOUR MARRIAGE. IT LETS EACH OTHER KNOW YOU CARE AND ARE CONCERNED.

YOU NEED AGAPE LOVE IN YOUR MARRIAGE. THIS HELPS HEAL WOUNDS. HOW BLESSED YOU

ARE TO KNOW YOU HAVE A MATE WHO TRIES TO BE UNDERSTANDING AND IS WILLING TO MAKE SACRIFICES FOR THE SAKE OF THE FAMILY.

A Partnership Marriage

It has been said the best way to a HAPPY MARRIAGE is to have a PARTNERSHIP MARRIAGE — 50-50! Each one has certain jobs and responsibilities. I disagree with this 110 percent. Marriage is not a partnership; it is a relationship! Yes, a partnership carries with it duties and responsibilities, but a partnership can be bought out by one party at any time. A partnership can be dissolved at any time. The love you need to hold a marriage together is seldom found in a partnership.

Marriage is a RELATIONSHIP. In a relationship the husband may carry 75-80 percent of the load some days because the wife is sick or the children need special attention or the wife may be a working member of the family. Why does a husband, willingly, jump in and do 75-80 percent of the load? It is very simple. He is understanding, he is willing to make a few sacrifices for the family, he cares and is concerned. He LOVES HIS WIFE! This is Philio and Agape Love at work and this is the kind of love that holds a family together. You don't find this kind of love in a partnership!

In a relationship the wife may some days have to carry 75-80 percent of the load because the husband is sick or the husband is committed to be out of town because of his work. Why does a wife, willingly, jump right in and carry this load? It is very simple, isn't it? She LOVES HER HUSBAND! NOT WITH A KIND OF LOVE YOU FIND IN A PARTNERSHIP! She loves him with a kind of love you find in a GOOD MARRIAGE RELATIONSHIP.

This is a love that is always filled with caring, concern, understanding and sacrifice.

Don't ever allow someone to talk you into a PARTNERSHIP MARRIAGE! Tell them you want a MARRIAGE

RELATIONSHIP that carries with it a visible kind of love that is filled with PHILIO AND AGAPE LOVE.

If you want a happy and joyful marriage, enter into marriage with this kind of MARRIAGE RELATIONSHIP!

MARRIAGE AND FAMILY LIFE

What kind of a family life are you going to have in your marriage relationship? How close is your family going to be? How close are your friends going to be? How are your jobs going to affect your family life? How will your hobbies and free time affect your family life? How will drinking and drugs affect your family life? How will anything you do affect your family life?

Everything I have mentioned can have a good or a drastic effect on your marriage. I have discovered the vast majority of marriages will fall into one of the following categories.

- **STRAIGHT-LINE MARRIAGE**
- **RAGING-TRIANGLE MARRIAGE**
- **A LOPSIDED-TRIANGLE MARRIAGE**
- **A DISASTROUS-TRIANGLE MARRIAGE**
- **AN IDEAL-TRIANGLE MARRIAGE**
- **AN IDEAL-DIAMOND MARRIAGE**
- **A LOPSIDED-DIAMOND MARRIAGE**

If you study each of these approaches to marriage you are going to discover you belong to one or close to one.

```
H •━━━━━━━━━• W
```

The Straight-Line Marriage

This solid line between husband and wife represents equal loyalty and love. The straight-line marriage is one that tells parents, family, friends, loved ones and the whole world all we need to make our marriage a success is ourselves. We don't care how our family, friends, loved ones or anyone else feels. They say, "THIS IS OUR MARRIAGE AND WE DON'T NEED ANYBODY'S HELP!"

To say the least, this places a tremendous strain on family relations. You would have to experience this kind of a marriage as I have to know the heartbreak it can bring to loved ones. Yet there are those who boldly CHOSE THIS KIND OF A MARRIAGE RELATIONSHIP. Without all three kinds of love mentioned in the previous chapter from both parties, this marriage is filled with trouble.

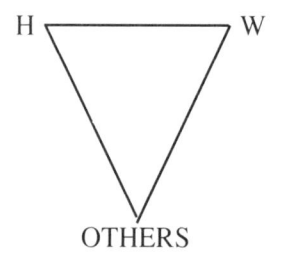

```
H ╲────────╱ W
   ╲      ╱
    ╲    ╱
     ╲  ╱
      ╲╱
    OTHERS
```

Raging-Triangle Marriage

In this relationship the husband, wife, family, and friends all have a dominate say as to how this family is to be run. In this relationship the husband's family demands his presence at activities, family functions, and in making decisions. Likewise, the wife's family demands her presence at activities, family functions, and in making decisions. If you want to see a family on the move, this would be a good one to watch. You are running in three directions at the same time. The wife is making suggestions along with her family and his family and him. Holidays and special days can be quite an experience when everyone seems to have a say in what is going on. The husband and wife seldom do what they would like to do because family and friends seem to have as much say as they do in their marriage. This is why there is a solid line on all three sides. To say the least this is not the ideal marriage; however, it is amazing how many families choose this style of marriage.

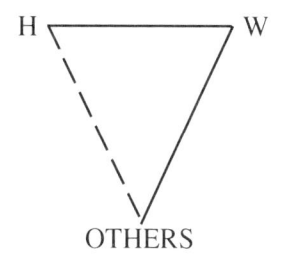

```
        H ─────── W
          \     /
           \   /
            \ /
             V
           OTHERS
```

A Lopsided-Triangle Marriage

The broken lines represent a loving relationship without any dominance or control from family or friends, BUT ONLY FROM ONE PARTY. The other party, not all the time, but most of the time, still allows family ties and friends to control what goes on in this marriage relationship. It could well be that in this kind of marriage one party is controlling the money or makes all the decisions. If you would refer back to part B under EROS, you will discover the man's relationship with his father in buying that car is like this.

THAT YOUNG MAN DISCOVERED IF HE DIDN'T WANT TO SLEEP WITH HIS DAD HE'D BETTER INCLUDE HIS WIFE IN ANY DECISION MAKING POLICIES OF THAT FAMILY.

A LOPSIDED-TRIANGLE is not the best marriage possible. In fact it is one that is doomed to fail within six months to 30 years. The broken line party becomes nothing except a TAG ALONG. A TAG ALONG will begin to feel as if everything and everyone else comes before him/her. He or she will just have to TAG ALONG and do what everybody else wants to do. The TAG ALONG'S thoughts, ideas, suggestions and feelings don't seem to count. A COLDNESS begins to set in on the part of the TAG ALONG and sooner or later this person will seek to get out of this kind of relationship.

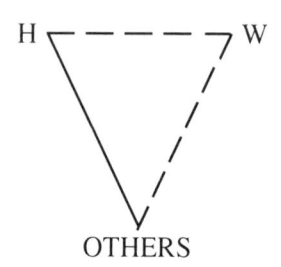

```
H ⌐ — — — ⌐ W
 \         /
  \       /
   \     /
    \   /
     \ /
      V
    OTHERS
```

A Disastrous-Triangle Marriage

I have known this marriage to last from six weeks to six months. Very seldom does it last much longer. What is so unusual about this kind of marriage?

Very simply, one party is tied to former things or persons that mean more to them than their mates. I have seen everything from drugs, sporting events, family ties and extra-marital affairs fit into this category. A bride can be so tied to her family that she always goes to her family instead of her husband when things are to be done and decisions made. A bride or a bridegroom can be so tied to drugs or alcohol that this will come before his/her mate. One can be so involved with athletics that athletics always comes before his/her mate. Affairs begin and before long the affair always come before the mate. In this kind of relationship one party never, never has a chance to share any input into what is going on because the other one is always dependent upon others, or something, more than his/her mate.

The big difference between this and the LOPSIDED-TRIANGLE is that this party is BOLD AND BRAZEN ABOUT IT! Even this behavior can be hidden for a while, but not for long. A young man married six weeks seeks out the pastor who married him. Tears are running down his cheeks as he talks. He has filed for DIVORCE! His Bride, from day one of their marriage, never gave him a fighting chance as a husband. The Bride and her mother made all the decisions in that home. After colors were chosen for redecorating their home, the Bride's mother changed them to her liking. The Bride always checked with mother after they had decided to eat out or go to a movie. Mother always had a better place to eat or a better movie to see. After deciding where to spend their vacation, mother decided a better place to go. The mother even changed menus agreed on by the couple. In other words, the bride and her mother decided who, what, where, why, and how everything was to be done. This kind of MARRIAGE RELATIONSHIP IS DOOMED FROM THE VERY BEGINNING. It is merely a matter of how much suffering and agony one party wants to go through before it is over. This young man, after six weeks, was so cold and bitter there was NO WAY TO SAVE THIS MARRIAGE.

A professional man lived with a woman several years. No marriage took place. In time he met a young, beautiful woman and swept her off her feet. He told her everything she wanted to hear and before long they were married. In six weeks they were separated. The reason for their separation was he was still carrying on an affair with his former lover. Then he went back to his wife and promised he would be a faithful husband. Within three months the wife discovered that her husband believed he was God's gift to women, and he had several women besides his former lover he was seeing. He admitted this to his wife when confronted. This DISASTROUS-TRIANGLE is one where there is a CON ARTIST as a mate. BELIEVE ME! THIS DOES HAPPEN! When it does, the naive, innocent party is almost destroyed. They do not want to believe what they know. They are crushed and sometimes come close to destruction. These are the ones who need the medication while the CON ARTIST goes along his happy old way.

Parents who have discovered, the hard way, that their child is on drugs learn they can even be CONNED by their own children. It happens with grandparents as well. Parents or grandparents can do everything for a child or grandchild and then discover a child will lie, cheat or steal from them and use them to their own advantage. Think how heartbreaking this is to parents and grandparents. Then remember this can happen even within marriages. Do you really know the person you are marrying or are you being swept off your feet with a lot of emotion and things you like to hear? You want marriage to be happy and a long lasting experience. You want it filled with love, harmony and peace. This is why you should seriously give the IDEAL-TRIANGLE AND IDEAL-DIAMOND A FIGHTING CHANCE.

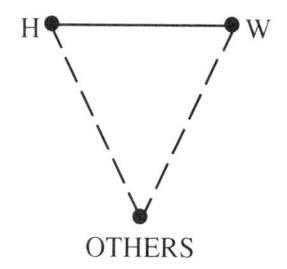

```
      H●─────────●W
        \       /
         \     /
          \   /
           \ /
            ●
         OTHERS
```

The Ideal-Triangle Marriage

THE IDEAL-TRIANGLE HAS A BROKEN LINE FROM BOTH HUSBAND AND WIFE TO THEIR FAMILIES and FRIENDS OR SOMETHING. In this relationship the husband is telling his wife, "You and your needs come before my family and friends and other things." Here the wife is telling her husband, "You and your needs come before my family and my friends or other things."

One of the scriptures used in many weddings is "FOR THIS REASON A MAN SHALL LEAVE HIS FATHER AND MOTHER AND BE JOINED TO HIS WIFE AND THEY SHALL BE NO LONGER TWO BUT ONE. TRULY WHOM GOD HATH JOINED TOGETHER, LET NO MAN PUT ASUNDER." (Matthew 19:5)

In the IDEAL-TRIANGLE MARRIAGE neither husband or wife can be "married" to their family and friends or other things and to each other at the same time. This does not mean you cannot have a wonderful relationship with your family and friends. It does mean, however, the immediate family comes first. Mom, dad, sisters, brothers, cousins, friends and things never control your lives and the lives of your family.

In this relationship a husband looks lovingly into the eyes of his wife and declares, "MY LOVE FOR YOU COMES FIRST, BEFORE MY FAMILY AND FRIENDS AND EVERYTHING ELSE." A wife looks lovingly into the eyes of her husband and declares, "MY LOVE FOR YOU COMES FIRST, BEFORE MY FAMILY, FRIENDS, AND EVERYTHING ELSE."

In this relationship your family and friends may want you to do something with them. You know you and your mate have already made plans for that time. You tell your family or friends you cannot make it because you and your mate have already made plans that cannot be broken. PLEASE REMEMBER IMMEDIATE FAMILY PLANS SHOULD NEVER BE BROKEN WITHOUT BOTH AGREEING.

The IDEAL-TRIANGLE MARRIAGE is what causes love to grow between husband and wife. Here is where a home really begins to experience LOVE, JOY, PEACE AND HAPPINESS. Every time a husband tells a family member or friend he can not do what that person would like to have him do because his wife and he have plans made and his wife comes first, SHE IS GOING TO SHOWER HIM WITH EROS LOVE! NOTHING CAUSES A WIFE TO FEEL BETTER THAN KNOWING AND EXPERIENCING SHE COMES FIRST IN HER HUSBAND'S LIFE.

Every time a wife tells a friend or a family member she cannot do what that person wants to do because her husband and she have plans made and he comes first, THAT HUSBAND IS GOING TO SHOWER THAT WIFE WITH EROS LOVE. NOTHING MAKES A HUSBAND FEEL BETTER THAN KNOWING AND EXPERIENCING HE COMES FIRST IN HIS WIFE'S LIFE!

```
      GOD
       •
      / \
     /   \
    /     \
   /       \
  /         \
 H•←————————•W
  \         /
   \       /
    \     /
     \   /
      \ /
       •
     OTHERS
       OR
     THINGS
```

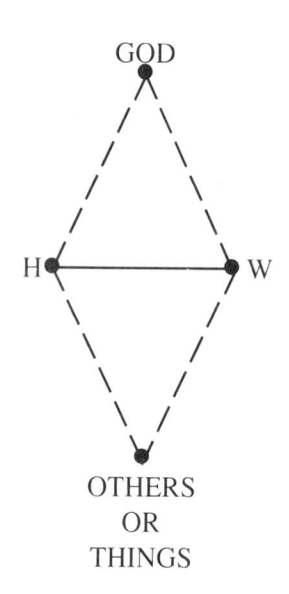

The Ideal-Diamond Marriage

IF YOU WANT TO HAVE THE HAPPIEST MARRIAGE YOU CAN FIND HERE ON EARTH, HERE IT IS! This is the IDEAL-TRIANGLE with an added ideal triangle at the top making it an IDEAL-DIAMOND MARRIAGE RELATIONSHIP. Here we find the husband and wife always reminding themselves that each other comes before family, friends, hobbies and all other things. HERE WE SEE EROS, PHILIO AND AGAPE LOVE WORKING TOGETHER IN A MARVELOUS WAY. If we take time to review that IDEAL-DIAMOND, we can begin to see why peace, harmony, love and joy can happen in this kind of a relationship.

IN THE IDEAL-DIAMOND MARRIAGE RELATIONSHIP we have a broken line going to the top and bottom from both husband and wife. In this relationship the top of the diamond is GOD AND THE CHURCH. The bottom of the diamond is family, friends, hobbies, habits and all other elements. God and the church even understand if there is sickness, or your job causes you to work on the Sabbath, or you are on vacation in the wilderness and you may not be able to worship in a church building on the Sabbath day. That is why there is a broken line between you and GOD AND THE CHURCH. There are sound reasons why even God understands you may not be present in a worship service. The top half of the DIAMOND really can make the bottom half of the DIAMOND WORK.

On Sunday morning a couple drives into the church parking lot. As soon as they open the car doors, you notice they are "BARKING" at each other. One walks ten feet ahead of the other although they are still "BARKING" at each other all the way into the church building. Once inside the church they are all smiles and greet other people with "hi's" and "hello's." When church is over, this couple is walking arm in arm, hand in hand, as they come out of church and all the way to their car. If you look closely, you may see this husband "patting" his wife on the bottom all the way to the car. They give each other a kiss before they enter the car, and they snuggle together as they leave the church parking lot.

What in the world has happened to turn this couple around? Why aren't they "barking" at each other as they leave? The top half of this DIAMOND PLAYED THE PART OF BRINGING THIS COUPLE BACK TOGETHER. Maybe it was during the singing of a hymn, maybe it was during the time of prayer, or possibly, it happened during the sermon. I have known it to happen during the time of SILENT MEDITATION. God and the church can play a vital part in making your MARRIAGE RELATIONSHIP THE HAPPIEST YOU CAN HAVE HERE ON EARTH. The Diamond Marriage Relationship can really help and cause the IDEAL-TRIANGLE MARRIAGE RELATIONSHIP TO WORK! OH, HOW BLESSED ARE HUSBANDS AND WIVES WHO TRY TO LIVE WITHIN THIS IDEAL-DIAMOND MARRIAGE RELATIONSHIP.

```
        GOD
         /\
        /  \
       /    \
      /      \
   H •────────• W
      \      /
       \    /
        \  /
         \/
         •
       OTHERS
```

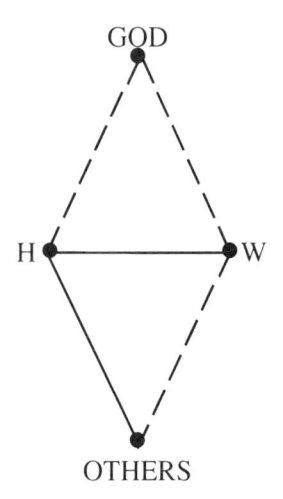

A Lopsided-Diamond Marriage

A LOPSIDED-DIAMOND MARRIAGE is a LOPSIDED-TRIANGLE MARRIAGE with a new dimension added. The only difference is a third party enters the picture who gives strength and help to the tag along. I have heard countless numbers of people say, "The only thing that saved our marriage was God and the church. Here is where I felt loved and accepted and treated like a somebody. Here is where I received the strength and help I needed to get through those tough and trying days." Some have said, "Here is where I received the strength to carry the cross I have to bear!"

Many a parent has stated, "If it weren't for God, we would never have made it!" Many a sick person has said, "If it weren't for God I would never have made it!" So many still say, "What do people do who have no God to turn to?"

Likewise, in a marriage, the LOPSIDED-DIAMOND TELLS US WE HAVE GOD TO HELP US THROUGH TROUBLED AND DIFFICULT TIMES. "There is nothing going to happen to us today that God and I can't handle!" (Paraphrase, 2 Corinthians 1:3-4)

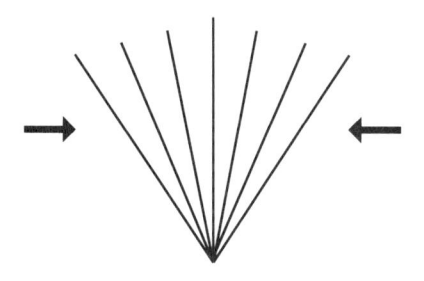

The Wedge

The WEDGE is a result of someone having his/her feelings hurt! If you have ever heard someone say he/she is "CRUSHED" because her/his husband or wife did or said something you are aware how the WEDGE CAN BEGIN! It can happen with shouts of anger and everyone is aware someone is unhappy. Most of the time it happens in SILENCE. You put it in the back of your mind, BUT YOU NEVER FORGET IT!

In the WEDDING CEREMONY those beautiful words of scripture were read: "LOVE IS PATIENT AND KIND. LOVE IS NOT JEALOUS OR BOASTFUL, IT IS NOT ARROGANT OR RUDE. LOVE DOES NOT INSIST UPON ITS OWN WAY. LOVE DOES NOT REJOICE AT WRONG, BUT REJOICES IN THE RIGHT. LOVE BEARS ALL THINGS, BELIEVES ALL THINGS, HOPES ALL THINGS, ENDURES ALL THINGS. LOVE NEVER ENDS." (1 Corinthians 13:4-8a)

Those words of scripture sound WONDERFUL! The WEDDING CEREMONY WAS BEAUTIFUL! The music was great! Everyone did an exceptional job at the WEDDING and RECEPTION! In most marriages a WEDGE APPEARS in a marriage relationship between a husband and wife. IT IS JUST ONE OF THOSE THINGS THAT HAPPEN!

This happens to a greater degree in the STRAIGHT-LINE, RAGING-TRIANGLE, LOPSIDED- AND DISASTROUS-TRIANGLE MARRIAGES; much more so than in the IDEAL-TRIANGLE AND THE IDEAL-DIAMOND MARRIAGES!

How does the WEDGE GET STARTED? HOW DOES IT WORK? HOW CAN IT BE DESTRUCTIVE? HOW CAN IT BE CORRECTED? Let's take a look at it and see. A family has children involved in a program. It is on the calendar and both parties plan to attend. On the day of the program the husband tells his wife, "You take them! I'm going to stay home and watch the ball game on TV." The wife doesn't say a word in front of the children, but she is crushed because BALL GAMES COME BEFORE THE FAMILY. (Remember the bottom of the triangle included family, friends, jobs, hobbies, and ball games.)

Time passes and the husband and wife agree to purchase new drapes for the living room. The husband comes home with new fishing equipment and informs the wife the curtains will have to wait. He spent the money for curtains on new fishing equipment!

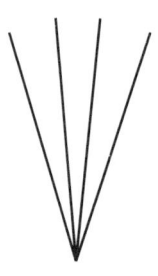

Again the wife is crushed because FISHING COMES BEFORE THE FAMILY! She can scream and shout but, usually she does a SLOW BURN and another wedge is found in the husband-wife relationship.

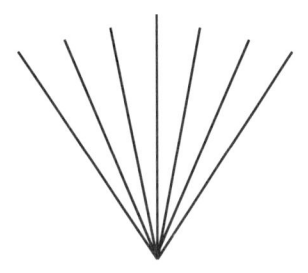

Then comes the day a relative is to be married. They have both planned to attend. On the day of the wedding the husband informs his wife, "I'm going to play golf today, you go to the wedding!" Need I say any more? The wife is again crushed because the husband thinks more of GOLF THAN A RELATIVE. Yes, another WEDGE IS DRIVEN BETWEEN THEM.

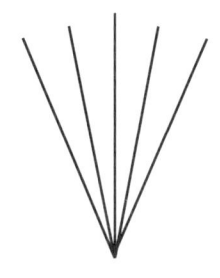

A wife and husband are dining out for their anniversary. As soon as they arrive at the restaurant, the husband sees some of his buddies. He excuses himself for a minute to talk to his buddies and winds up having a couple of drinks with them. He cannot understand why his wife is upset when he returns. SHE IS CRUSHED! HIS BUDDIES COME BEFORE HER! (The bottom of that triangle again!) Another wedge is driven between this husband and wife.

COLDNESS

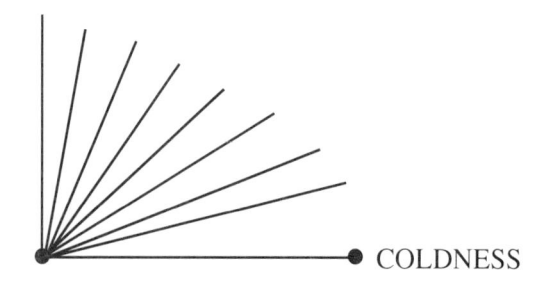

It happens with husbands and wives! Little wedges slip in and life goes on UNTIL ONE FEELS A COLDNESS COME OVER THEM WHERE THEY DO NOT EVEN WANT TO BE IN THE SAME ROOM WITH THE ONE THEY MARRIED! This is the time one declares NO MORE! NO MORE HURTS, BEING PUT LAST, BEING TAKEN FOR GRANTED! THEY WANT OUT!

A counselor had a wife come to the office one day and she said, "You have to talk to my husband! He filed for a DIVORCE! I never dreamed there was anything wrong!" After a long talk with the husband, the counselor discovered they had discussed a divorce many times before. Immediately the counselor discovered a LOPSIDED-TRIANGLE marriage! The husband's suggestions, ideas and dreams too many times had to be discussed and approved by the wife and her boss. His wife and her boss always knew the best places to go and things to do. This husband even felt like his wife's boss had an upper hand in the clothing his wife wore. Every time his wife and her boss SUGGESTED places to go and things to do, another little wedge was driven between them. Many times this was done in silence, but it was never forgotten. The husband came to the point where he strongly suspected his wife and her boss were having an affair. AFTER SEVERAL YEARS OF MARRIAGE THEIR WEDGE LOOKED SOMETHING LIKE THIS.

COLDNESS

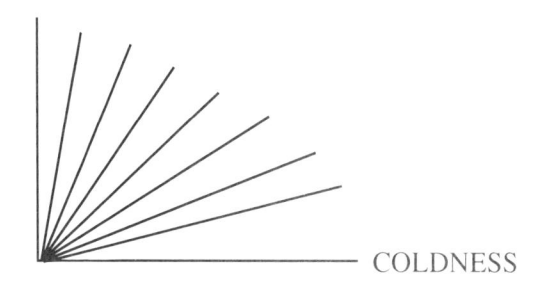

When the wife was confronted with all of these WEDGES, all she could say was, "I didn't know those things bothered him." It was too late! NO ONE COULD REKINDLE THAT FIRE THAT BROUGHT THEM TOGETHER! The husband became cold and bitter and longed to be free of that marriage.

Another example of that wedge is a husband who never does anything with the family and spends money foolishly at the expense of the family. The husband always puts himself first and his wife last. The husband always gets whatever he wants and leaves his wife to go without. Her wedge will be similar to the husband we just discussed!

When this wife filed for divorce, the husband could not understand WHY. When asked, "Do you remember when you spent money for this, this, and that AND YOUR WIFE WAS ALWAYS GOING WITHOUT? DO YOU REMEMBER WHEN YOU TREATED YOUR WIFE LIKE THIS, THIS, THIS AND THAT?" His answer was, "I thought she forgot all those things!"

NO! NO! NO! Very few of us are so GOD-LIKE we forgive and forget that easily. So often that WEDGE CONTINUES TO GROW AND GROW AND THE COLDNESS BECOMES GREATER AND GREATER UNTIL YOU CRY OUT, "I CAN'T TAKE IT ANY MORE. I WANT OUT." AND YOU DON'T EVEN WANT TO BE SEEN WITH THAT PERSON YOU MARRIED.

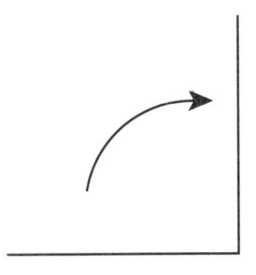

A Solution To The Wedge Problem!

FIRST it takes all three kinds of love — EROS, PHILIO, AND AGAPE — to bring the WEDGE under control. As soon as one feels the wedge get started (you can usually feel it because EROS love is not at its best), RIGHT THEN, RIGHT THEN IS THE TIME FOR THE HUSBAND AND WIFE TO SAY, "WE HAVE A PROBLEM!" If PHILIO AND AGAPE LOVE is missing from your marriage, your chances of putting that marriage back together is ALMOST IMPOSSIBLE!

Use that PHILIO and AGAPE LOVE for one another to solve any problems as soon as possible. Work as hard as you can to close that WEDGE and become the people OR EVEN BETTER PEOPLE THAN YOU WERE ON YOUR WEDDING DAY!

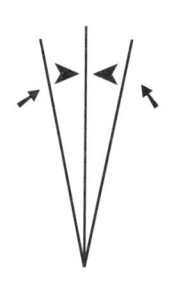

WEDDING PLANS

Weddings can be a blessing, filled with rejoicing, tears of happiness, something grand and glorious. Many can also be frustrating, with tears of disappointment and moments of sadness. To help eliminate this, a wedding information page and guidelines for a traditional wedding are included at the close of this chapter.

Items 1-7 concern the BRIDE. It is very helpful for the clergy to know if the Bride is divorced, widowed or single. Are there any children from previous marriages? The telephone number of home and work are important in case there is a conflict in the pastor's schedule for a consultation or information needs to be passed on about an organist, soloist etc. The parents' names are important, and knowing if they are married, widowed, divorced or remarried can save a lot of embarrassment. Plans can be made concerning seating and other arrangements in cases concerning divorced or separated parents.

Items 8-14 concern the BRIDEGROOM. The information is identical to the Bride's.

Items 15-16 are general housekeeping items.

Item 17 concerns your wedding expenses. Make sure you know your expenses up front to avoid embarrassment.

Item 18 relates to your Marriage License. Never wait until the last few days to think about your license. You can make arrangements up to 60 days before your wedding.

Item 19 concerns the rehearsal date. It is not only important to the clergy and organist, but all participants. The time and the place should be made very clear. Nothing is more embarrassing than getting lost or coming in late. The time of the rehearsal is often not made clear and then a rehearsal has to start 30 minutes or an hour late because someone forgot or didn't know.

Item 20 concerns the rehearsal dinner which is sometimes a difficult situation. A map and time for the dinner would be wise if you have strangers to your community in your wedding party. Following someone when you are traveling several miles in a city can be most difficult and confusing.

Item 21 is about the wedding date and hour. These are things you don't assume everyone knows. The date and hour should be mentioned several times.

Item 22 notes the place of the rehearsal and wedding. This is not always a church. Churches sometimes are not easy to locate if you are a stranger to a community. Good directions are always important.

Item 23 relates to fees. Churches and ministers vary as to when you must pay your fees. It is always good advice to pay all fees ahead of time. This leaves the wedding day for the wedding. Running around to find people after a wedding is over to settle your accounts is usually the last thing a new bride and groom are thinking about.

•Sentinel. This person could be a very important part of your wedding party. Many times clothing, jewelry, billfolds, pocketbooks, shoes, and miscellaneous items are left behind in the Bride and Bridegroom's dressing rooms. Try to have someone not involved in your wedding party to double check all the rooms used to be sure all personal items are taken with you. The last things a WEDDING PARTY thinks about after the wedding are the dressing rooms. There are places to go and there are things to do.

Items 24-32 concern the wedding party. 24-28 are standard for most weddings. It is, however, very important to know which ushers or members of the wedding party are going to seat the mothers. Groomsmen may be your ushers or you may have special groomsmen PLUS your regular ushers. Most times they are the same. Do you wish to have anyone participate in your wedding as a reader of scripture or poetry? Which ushers will light the candles? Are you going to have ringbearers or flowergirls and others? To know all this before your rehearsal is very important for the clergy and the parties being married. The time you save at your rehearsal is amazing.

Wedding Music And Wedding Trifles

Items 33-34 relate to Wedding Music. Wedding music is usually played one-half hour before the wedding. You have the right to choose every number the organist plays or a soloist sings during this time. You also have the right to have the organist choose traditional wedding music to be played during this time, and you choose the soloist's music and the music for the mothers and the wedding party. Think about it! During that one-half hour before your wedding you will not hear any of the music; neither will your parents or your wedding party. Most church organists have a good command of wedding music, and if they choose the general wedding music you can concentrate on the special music used in your wedding.

Items 35-36 relate to the mothers. What music do you want played as the mothers are seated? A word about grandparents being seated: The grandparents are seated before the mothers. The Groom's grandparents are always seated before the Bride's grandparents and the Groom's mother is always seated before the Bride's mother. Leaving the church, the Bride's mother is always ushered out first.

Item 37 relates to the wedding music you want played as the Wedding Party comes down the aisle.

Item 38 relates to the wedding music the bride wants played as she comes down the aisle. It can be traditional or other.

Item 39 relates to the recessional the wedding party will use as they leave the church.

BE AWARE! SOME CHURCHES, PASTORS, AND PRIESTS TELL YOU WHAT MUSIC CAN BE USED!

Items 40-41 are housekeeping items but essential to know. Are you going to use an aisle runner? Which ushers will unroll it? Are you going to have a Unity Candle as part of your wedding? What music do you want used during the candle service?

Item 42 relates to the person presenting the bride.

Item 43 relates to the rings used in a wedding. No rings are required. One may be used, but usually two are used.

Item 44 relates to where the reception will be held. For informational use.

Items 45-50 are housekeeping items. The organist you choose is most important. Make sure, if you are not using the church's organist, the one you want can handle the church organ. The name of the florist assists in eliminating a mix up. We have had flowers delivered to wrong churches, and only because we knew the name of the florist were we able to solve the problem before the wedding. Photographers should know the rules of the church. Very few churches will allow a photographer to roam freely during a wedding to take pictures. They can take away so much from a wedding by having all the attention given to them rather than the couple being married. Most photographers use good common sense. The soloist and the organist must practice together; so names and telephone numbers are important. If you are leaving flowers or items at the church to be used by the church, most churches will want to recognize this with proper credit. Videos are very popular. Most churches have places for the video equipment. Some photographers hesitate taking pictures if video people are situated so as to be included in wedding pictures.

What Kind Of A Wedding Are You Planning?

A suggested TRADITIONAL style wedding is given for you to study. In most churches you will have a choice of including things in your wedding. AGAIN THERE ARE CHURCHES THAT TELL YOU WHAT KIND OF A

WEDDING YOU CAN HAVE RATHER THAN YOU DECIDING YOUR STYLE OF WEDDING. In the suggested form the * indicates options which you may include or may not include. This is up to you.

Most churches will allow a few changes and additions to your wedding. Be sure to keep track of your counseling notes.

We trust your wedding will be a beautiful and wonderful occasion. May God Bless you and may your lives always be filled with LOVE, JOY AND PEACE.

WEDDING INFORMATION

1. WOMAN'S FULL NAME _____
2. Status: _____(D) _____(W) _____(S) Children _____
3. Birth _____
4. Address _____
5. Telephone: Work _____Home _____
6. Parents' Name _____M D W R
7. Address _____

8. MAN'S FULL NAME _____
9. Status: _____(D) _____(W) _____(S) Children _____
10. Birth _____
11. Address _____
12. Telephone: Work _____Home _____
13. Parents' Name _____M D W R
14. Address _____

15. Dates to meet with the Pastor _____
16. Church Member _____ Attender _____ Friend _____
17. Minimum Fees:
    1. Church _____ 5. Church Vocalist _____
    2. Organist _____ 6. Candelabra_____
    3. Custodian _____ 7. Fellowship Rm. _____
    4. Pastor _____ 8. Birdseed or rice, extra
18. License may be procured up to 60 days prior to wedding.
19. Rehearsal Date _____Hour _____Place _____
20. Rehearsal Dinner Date _____Hour _____Place _____
21. Wedding Date _____Hour _____
22. Place _____
23. **Marriage License and fees to be taken care of before or at the rehearsal**
    * Sentinel _____Double check rooms to see that no personal items are left behind.

WEDDING PARTY

24. Maid of Honor _____
25. Matron of Honor _____
26. Best Man _____
27. Bridesmaids _____
   _____

28. Ushers _____
   _____

29. Seating Bride's Mom _____
    Seating Groom's Mom _____
30. Groomsmen _____
   _____

31. Reader _____ Lighting Candles _____
32. Other attendants _____

WEDDING MUSIC & TRIFLES

Music:
33. Prelude music (optional) _____
34. Selected _____
   _____

35. Mothers Lighting Candles _____
36. Music for Mothers _____
37. Music for Bridal Party _____
38. Music for Bride _____ Traditional _____ Selected
39. Recessional _____ Traditional _____ Selected
40. Aisle Runner: Yes _____ No _____ Who _____
41. Unity Candle: Yes _____ No _____ Music _____
42. Who presents the bride in marriage? _____
43. Will you use one ring? _____ or two rings? _____
44. Reception _____
45. Organist _____ 48. Soloist _____
46. Florist _____ 49. Credit _____
47. Photographer _____ 50. Video _____

45

What Kind Of Wedding? | Changes And Additions

Ascription
* Scripture or Poetry
Address to Congregation
* Giving of the Bride
* Greeting of the Father
Address to Bride and Bridegroom
Declaration of Intentions
* Scripture and Homily (your choice or pastor's choice)
Prayer or Solo
Vows
Rings
* Unity Candle
Prayers
Union
* Introduction

* Indicates these are options

General Questions About The Wedding:

Pastoral Counseling Notes:

SERIOUS THINGS TO CONSIDER BEFORE DIVORCE

What causes DIVORCE? Sometimes it seems as if there are as many reasons as people. A few of the most popular reasons are UNFAITHFULNESS, MONEY, DRUGS, LACK OF CONCERN, BEING MISTREATED, GROWING APART, DIFFERENT INTERESTS, HANDLING OF CHILDREN, SEX, IN-LAWS, THE GRASS IS GREENER ON THE OTHER SIDE, POOR HOUSEKEEPER, TELEVISION, BALL GAMES, BEER AND DRUG PARTIES, FISHING, BOATING, RECREATION, NO TIME FOR ONE ANOTHER, POOR COMMUNICATION, and the list goes on. As we have stated earlier, the one overused by professionals, "YOU CAN FALL IN LOVE, YOU CAN FALL OUT OF LOVE!"

So many times the only type of LOVE a couple has going into marriage is what we mentioned earlier, EROS LOVE. Without PHILIO LOVE and AGAPE LOVE in a marriage, it takes very little to go wrong and we are off to see the lawyers. I have been reminded by some judges that many lawyers are happy feeding upon the desire of the parties to inflict pain upon each other. Where is the care and concern? Where is the understanding and willingness to make sacrifices?

Many times I have had people come to me and confess they are having an affair. One of the above reasons is usually given as the reason the affair started. Many other times people will

tell counselors they are having marriage problems and later learn an affair has been going on with one of the parties. Certainly there are those who have problems who can work them out with a little help. SOMETIMES, regardless of the help, there is no hope to hold a family together. Many of these examples have been given in earlier chapters. Allow me to suggest there are serious things to consider before getting a DIVORCE. One way to seriously test the water:
 1. Make a list of everything you like about your present home.
 2. Make a list of everything you don't like about your present home.
 3. Make a list of everything you will not like about your divorce.
 4. Make a list of everything you will like about your divorce.

If you can be honest with these four questions you can start to make some serious considerations.

A man told a friend he was having an affair with a physical fitness instructor and said, "BOY IS IT EVER EXCITING!" The friend asked him to make a list of these four items just mentioned and give it some serious thought. This is what is looked like:

1. **Likes Present**
Wife is so-so
Love children
Finances great
Many friends
Good family life

2. **Dislikes Present**
Wife could be better

3. **Likes Future**
Gal is sexy
Great body
Athletic

4. **Dislikes Future**
Poor housekeeper
Poor mother
Bad finances
Bad habits

What do you think happened? Maybe you have heard the old story:

*Marriage is an institution and love is blind,
Therefore, marriage is an institution for the blind.*

He got his divorce and is learning the hard way, SEX is not the only thing that makes a happy marriage. As we mentioned earlier, SEX is the first thing you use to punish the one you married. When you say, "DON'T TOUCH ME! LEAVE ME ALONE!" you are using SEX to punish one another. What is this man going to do when his physical fitness instructor, who is so sexy and athletic, becomes angry with him and tells him, "DON'T TOUCH ME!" This is the only kind of love this man carried into this marriage. This is the only thing he really liked about her. Those four little questions gave us that message.

Many authors have told us that AFFAIRS grounded in SEX will not last long. The reason is so simple. SEX is the only weapon you have to really hurt the one who has wronged you. When you take that away for a day, a week or longer, what is left to hold that marriage together? Depression, anger, and getting even start to set in.

This is why it is so important to seriously seek counseling and face up to the future before you jump into a divorce. The scripture tells us before we do anything, we must "FIRST, COUNT THE COST!" So many times this is never done, and we jump "from the frying pan right into the fire!"

Not all divorces, but a good many of them, could be salvaged if some bullheaded and stubborn people would first consider some counseling and the cost factor (not necessarily money) before jumping into separation and divorce.

I have heard many times the chief reason for divorce is MONEY! If people only had money, their problems would be solved. There would be fewer problems and there would be fewer divorces. I DISAGREE WITH THIS PHILOSOPHY!

In many of the illustrations mentioned before and in today's world, people seeking divorce have plenty of money. I feel the chief cause of divorce is NOT UNDERSTANDING

THE MEANING OF LOVE! I mean PHILIO LOVE AND AGAPE LOVE! This love must be included in every marriage as well as EROS LOVE! Only when we see caring, concern, understanding, and sacrificial love will we see a love that can hold marriages together.

If I am a caring and concerned person, if I am filled with understanding and willing to make sacrifices, I will love my mate enough to sit down and work out all my money problems. I will work out all my problems before they become monstrous. It is when we don't put forth the effort to work things out we run into problems.

If caring, concern, understanding and sacrificial love are included in a marriage many of the problems of marriage could be helped or solved. I cannot begin to count the number of people I have counseled being married the second or third time. Most of them have never heard about PHILIO AND AGAPE LOVE. "If someone had only told us this before!" Some would have never married the first time and some would have never divorced.

After counseling people for marriages and taking them through this book, I have had some cancel their weddings. They have realized before their wedding there are going to be BIG, BIG PROBLEMS. TWO HAVE CANCELED THEIR WEDDINGS AFTER HAVING THEIR MARRIAGE LICENSES.

To have a happy marriage, make sure both of you understand the FULL MEANING OF LOVE! Both parties must understand this in order to have a happy and meaningful marriage relationship. Love and all that it means must be possessed by both!